HOW TO MANAGE OFFICE LIKE A PROFESSIONAL BOSS

2

Contents

Introduction

The position of office manager is evolving. There is no question in my mind. Before the corona virus epidemic began, the role was starting to change. However, the office manager's position is changing when one returns to a real or virtual workplace.

Office managers are no longer responsible for buying office supplies, fixing broken printers, or making sure staff washes their dishes after lunch. Currently, they are crucial for employee satisfaction, safety, retention, and more.

This essay will examine the traits, abilities, and resources a fantastic office manager needs to succeed in their position this year and in the future.

Being able to manage a cubicle is vital since it may assist create a productive and enjoyable work environment for your staff and can position them for success. Using sound management strategies may help you enhance your office space and boost the success of your business, whether you organize your workspace or assist in the growth and training of team members' talents. This essay will explain the value of effective office administration and provide you with a list of practical advice.

It often relies on you as the office manager to keep things operating as smoothly as possible. But managing an office effectively may be a bit challenging at times when you add a group of people with various personalities, a variety of office supplies and software, and an endless number of distractions. However, none of this may prohibit you. In fact, it should serve as inspiration to maintain a clean workplace!

A multitude of responsibilities must be juggled while running an office. workplace managers maintain the workplace operating efficiently from day to day, week to week, month to month, and year to year. There are several aspects to take into account on a daily or broad scale. Office budgeting, inventory management, seating and design, new hire on boarding, record keeping, and other tasks may all be found on an office manager's to-do list.

Here are some office management suggestions to keep things moving smoothly if you want to supervise an office effectively and improve both your leadership and management skills.

Typical duties for an office supervisor position include the following:

The use of technology and software to maximize efficiency in office operations.

- Manage offline and online filing systems.

- Establish and maintain workplace budgets.

- Keep the office layout in good shape and perform any required repairs.

- When the front desk personnel is absent or ill, arrange for additional assistance.

- Answer client questions and grievances.

- Examine workplace safety and make any necessary updates.

A New Definition of Office Management

The role of an office manager is now more complicated and dynamic than ever before due to changes in technology, business structures, and working conditions in general.

Workplace managers still oversee a fixed, physical workplace where a core team of workers work during regular business hours in many businesses. However, the work and the people that many office managers supervise are dispersed across several locations, time zones, and different sorts of workplaces (particularly those who work for technology businesses).

As a result, your job as an office manager is evolving at an unimaginably rapid rate. As a result of these quick changes, there are also new resources, tools, and obstacles that must be overcome. The skills necessary for you to thrive in your career and the tasks that you are given undoubtedly vary, even if your job title may not.

We'll discuss some of the changes you should expect during your office management career as well as some of the difficulties you'll probably encounter on a regular basis in this article. Additionally, regardless of what your "workplace" looks like, we'll talk about the undeniable importance of your position and provide you with the resources and encouragement you need to make a difference.

An office manager is what?

When we discuss office management, we are really discussing what makes an office productive. All office managers are responsible for planning, coordinating, and regulating office operations as well as keeping an eye on government oversight, labor regulations, and employee happiness. Office managers have a range of duties based on the demands of their firm.

Office management positions might vary depending on the industry, but these managers' fundamental responsibilities are often relatively similar. Office managers sometimes have the authority to recruit, dismiss, train, and promote personnel in addition to overseeing the efficient operation of a business' administrative functions, making ensuring that necessary supplies are available, and checking that office equipment is in good working condition.

Making Your Office A Positive Place to Work

Your employees' capacity and motivation to accomplish good job are predetermined by the physical environment they operate in. Our surroundings have a big influence on us as humans. We fill our houses with souvenirs and artifacts that inspire us or make us feel good. To feel more "at home," we adorn our automobiles and working environments.

Similar efforts are made in commercial locations to maintain a certain vibe. While stadiums and music halls are built to be visually stimulating, hotels and spas are designed to promote comfort and tranquilly. While restaurants might be dark, romantic, young, or cozy, medical facilities are designed to seem spotless and contemporary.

However, aesthetics alone won't be sufficient to convey the goals or mood of any setting. It's also important to consider how people behave towards one another, how the room is organized and set up, how well individuals perform there, and how respectful your atmosphere is. Poor customer service by hotel workers cannot be concealed by attractive artwork displayed on the walls. If tables are dirty or the eating area is crowded and close-knit, patrons will not appreciate a restaurant's attempt to create a cozy and quiet atmosphere. The environment matters.

Learning Office Management Techniques

These people, sometimes known as office personnel, coordinators, and or managers of office operations, are often the first people someone within or outside the company contacts. Their responsibilities are diverse and include anything from helping to onboard new workers to fostering a healthy work environment to acting as executive assistants.

As a consequence, an office manager's workload soon increases. In addition to preserving the usefulness and adaptability of the office space, they must manage worker actions travel, deadlines, and a long list of other things. There are many expectations put on an office manager's position, and many employees have different ideas of what that manager should really do.

Being an office manager is incredibly satisfying because you get to go above and beyond what others expect of you. You might assume personal accountability for and contribute significantly to the success of an organization and its employees.

While many of these locations are created with the customer in mind, the workplace should also take the employees' preferences and requirements into consideration. Because of their comfort and satisfaction, employees are more likely to work efficiently and provide high-quality service, both of which will please your clients. Three significant changes you can make to the work environment will support employee performance and enjoyment.

What is office management crucial?

Office management is crucial since it may improve staff productivity, help you make better use of your working hours, and raise the quality of work produced by your organization. You may improve your administrative abilities, foster a positive work environment, and raise staff morale by using effective office administration ideas and procedures.

Prepare the area.

Organizing your workspace may increase team productivity and foster a productive working atmosphere. There are various ways you may set up your workplace, including:

- establishing designated work areas for staff

- updating corporate filing procedures

- Adding labels to cubbies, drawers, and shelves

- Sorting project materials into storage boxes and folders after completion

- Keeping a note of the supplies you need to restock, such as staplers and printer ink.

When attempting to establish a positive work environment, cleaning your office space may also be quite useful. Consider making a plan that will serve as a reminder for you and your team to clean certain areas of the workplace during the working day. For instance, you could dust and clean the break room on Mondays and reorganize and sort the mail on Thursdays. Employee productivity may be increased and distractions reduced by maintaining a clean workspace.

Instead of reacting, prepare.

The day will go more smoothly if you take the time to prepare for it rather than improvising responses to situations as they arise. Making plans for the next day might help you priorities activities more effectively and reduce a portion of the stress and uncertainty that comes with everyday living.

Maintain current records

Keeping current business documents may be an important part of running your office. Your office may save time and help your team work more efficiently by keeping track of client contact data, updating payment information, and noting when your staff has previously contacted customers.

For instance, it may be beneficial for a sales associate to note the contact details of a new customer, the nature of the interaction, and if your team will need to get in touch with the client again throughout the future. The salesperson may record the details that are so another employee doesn't spend time calling the same customer again if the chat went well and the client is already contemplating purchasing from your business.

Being the company's best organized employee

For good reason, organizational and time management abilities are at the top of the list. It goes beyond just developing a new file system. A manager of an office must be aware of everyone's schedule in addition to their own. The position necessitates balancing daily operations with long-term company strategies, third-party suppliers, and coworkers. If organization skills are lacking, work will quickly mount up.

Create a filing method that is effective for you.

Even though the majority of filing is now digital, you nevertheless have to keep track of what is kept where. If the web-based system is confusing, devise a better filing system and implement it. To ensure that everyone is filing properly, make sure others are aware of the method as well.

Create Open Channels of Communication

Your coworkers may undoubtedly come to you as the office manager with a variety of demands, inquiries, or requests. You must establish effective channels of communication in order to receive and process these requests quickly.

Maintain a tidy and organized inbox. Ignoring emails or leaving things incomplete might result in major disorganization and missing emails. Always try to keep your inbox as orderly as you can. Make it obvious to your employees how they may ask you questions or make suggestions. Sure, a simple inquiry like "where are the extra pens" may be made in person, but larger requests must always be made in writing. By doing this, you create a record and ensure that nothing is forgotten. Establish rules for how to reach you at work, whether you prefer Slack, email, or another channel for communicating with your colleagues.

You may need to set aside some time to stop responding to requests from coworkers while we're on the subject of communication. Focus on your critical work at hand and attend to any fresh inquiries afterwards. Be explicit about your obligations and position if someone makes a request that you can't fulfill immediately or at all. It's OK to refuse or assign to someone else if it's not your responsibility.

Realize the appropriate aesthetic
There are various ways you may influence the appearance and feel of

your workplace, even if design decisions might not be entirely your own. There is a fine art to maintaining a workplace that feels pleasant to everyone, from placing fresh flowers at the front desk or asking for a flickering light to be changed, to everyday actions like setting meeting rooms to their original settings and hanging art on the walls. For inspiration, draw on the reputation of your business and the kinds of work that your employees perform.

If your brand is original and disruptive and you produce a lot of creative work, use bolder colors, contemporary decor, and inspiring details. Consider a minimalist approach with subdued tones and fewer visual distractions if your workplace is calm and your job is contemplative and studious.

Planning abilities

Office managers should be inherently good at planning. Your planning duties will include anything from setting up office meetings to assigning tasks. Organized planning is a crucial talent that any excellent office manager should possess, from planning long-term corporate operations to carrying out daily chores effectively.

Ability to manage

Administrative expertise should come naturally to an office manager. There's a strong probability you had previous administrative roles before you progressed to office manager. You would have developed a foundational level of administrative abilities in these roles, and you will continue to do so as you become used to your new job as office manager. You'll be in charge of maintaining and growing the corporate culture, as well as other personnel duties including assessing employee performance. You'll also be in charge of a variety of administrative activities inside the organization.

Leadership potential

The most important ability a manager needs is leadership; some individuals naturally possess it, while others don't. You may either lead your team and yourself blindly into catastrophe or you can be an excellent leader.

There are many different forms and sizes of leadership. In a corporate travel firm like Travel Perk, you might be in charge of managing the tasks of over 100 employees or you may work in a small team of six people. It all comes down to accepting accountability for everyone who works for you, no matter how many employees there may be.

Effective task delegation

It's important to delegate. When it comes to assigning duties, many managers have a tendency to give the majority of them to themselves or to one or two employees in particular, which is unfair to both them and the rest of the office team.

Prioritizing what has to be done and then relinquishing control are crucial. There is an issue if you are unable to achieve it. The manager's job may be strained and they may not be able to function effectively in other areas if they are unable to assign work.

Plan out your week.
You can manage time in order more effectively and priorities your tasks by creating a weekly schedule. Look through your upcoming deadlines, meetings, and other critical tasks and rank them in order of importance at the start of each week. Use the following categories when sorting:

- Stationary: Any meeting or employee evaluations with a

specified date are considered stationary activities. You often already have these tasks set for you, so it is difficult for you to change them. It's beneficial to do all of your stationary chores first, then arrange the rest of your workload around them.

- Top Priority: Tasks that need to be finished as soon as possible, usually by the end of the week, or on certain days within the next week, are considered top priorities. Sorting these tasks according to their due dates might help you complete them in the order of significance.
- Flexible: The final tasks you add to your calendar are often flexible activities. These

are often assignments that you don't have to do by the end of the week but that might help with a project or assignment that has a deadline coming up. Consider transferring your intended flexible activities to the next week if you can't fit them all into this one since you may have more time to finish them.

Become a master communicator

To succeed in an office manager position, you must possess great communication skills. Giving precise instructions, resolving problems, and avoiding errors all help. One of the few positions in a firm that has contact with everyone, from new hires to C-level executives, is that of the office manager. Make sure you have strong communication skills since it will make the job much simpler.

Be creative while resolving issues

The depth of industry expertise that an office supervisor develops over time is unmatched. They are essential to a company's ability to get through its most trying moments, and they all stem from strong problem-solving skills. The more time you spend in the role, the more seniority levels will come to you for guidance on difficult staff problems.

However, problem-solving doesn't end there. An office manager will often be given the duty of implementing a plan with little or no funding. Your ability to use your resources creatively and to go forward in the face of obstacles is a requirement of the position.

Maintain performance

If there is no work being done, what use is a workplace? The idea that the environment in which people work should be clear, distraction-free, and perhaps the very opposite of engaging was prevalent decades ago. Workers were supposed to remain in their designated regions and were isolated. Thankfully, things have changed. According to research, employees operate most effectively in environments that are appropriate for the sort of job being done. Maintaining spaces for workers to concentrate, gather, or take well-earned breaks should be given equal weight.

Ability to analyze

It's a good idea to improve your analytical abilities at any level of job. In order to help your business succeed as a manager in an office you'll need to be able to spot inefficiencies and provide remedies.

Computer expertise

For an office manager, having solid, useful computer skills is not only good but also required. You should be proficient enough to do daily computer activities including data input, sheet preparation, and presentation formatting with ease, accuracy, and efficiency. Software will probably be used by you for communication on a daily basis, video conferencing, and expenditure reporting.

Making decisions quickly

Are you able to make rapid decisions on the spot? As an office manager, there are several situations that could need a quick reaction. For instance, you could need to coordinate with the carrier whose schedule includes multiple big goods that need to be moved from the reception or arrange a last-minute office layout for an event taking place in the building.

There are choices to be taken, and they could result from unforeseen circumstances that have just materialized. An office manager may find it useful to make decisions quickly, especially in a hectic setting.

Adaptability to others

You'll probably have a never-ending to-do list as an office manager. Even with it in place, you still need to be able to give some flexibility. There will be jobs that must be completed by a certain date and others that will crop up at the last minute and ruin your plans.

Always try to be flexible when you can, and try to take each day as it comes. Because things won't always go as planned, it's wise to be adaptable while you can.

Assign tasks

Delegating duties to staff members and other people may improve your office's efficiency and production while enabling you to fulfill deadlines that are crucial. Consider breaking up a major project into smaller components and delegating them to various team members if you need to finish it quickly, for instance. They can do all of those little jobs at once, which will free you up to combine the work and data into a single coherent paper or report once they're finished.

Communicative and approachable

An essential component of the office manager's job is communication. After all, they will serve as one of the building's primary visible and interior faces. It's crucial to have a kind disposition.

Regardless of who they are, anybody needs to be able to

approach the manager of the workplace without feeling intimidated or as like they are bothering her. It's advantageous to be a people person in every sense of the term because of the wide variety of personality types, diversities, backgrounds, and most crucially, seniorities.

Create routines

In an office setting, establishing routines may aid in managing workflow, developing methods for processing client information, and reacting to certain situations. It might be beneficial for an individual or team member to have a regular person to contact if they require extra work after finishing their given chores or tasks. You may contribute to the development of a self-sufficient workflow that enables a team to work routinely throughout the day while freeing up your own time to focus on your own chores and projects by assigning that assignment to another team member.

It's also crucial to have routines in place so that work may still be produced and deadlines met in situations, such as when the office block is closed or the corporate network is inoperable. Having strong, established routines will help you resolve any workplace issues or disagreements, whether you backup office hard drives or have a framework in place to work remotely if required.

Be understanding

Each office manager must be able to comprehend and empathies with every member of the team. An office manager often acts as the voice of the vast majority of workers since they are an integral component of the team and have a thorough understanding of everyone's working conditions. To make sure that everyone is heard and understood, you'll need to be able to lead with charm and empathy.

A manager of an office often finds themselves on committees for health or beneficial initiatives. They must be capable of leading initiatives that need empathy, using a business perspective with compassion, and balancing expectations and reality.

Try to limit interruptions!

As an office manager, you will surely be addressing a zillion inquiries simultaneously while attempting to do your daily obligations. A timetable can help you arrange your time and actually reduce interruptions since you'll be better able to respond to them at certain times when you can give them your complete attention. Make sure to take advantage of the times you anticipate being the quietest. Shut the door, put your phone on silent, and stay focused.

Maintain the mood

Beyond appearance, the ethos of your workplace is determined by how people interact with one another, the attitudes and perspectives of your team, and the prominence of guiding principles like respect, trust, and innovation. What language do your folks use while conversing? What emotions and feelings do most individuals exhibit at work? Is it hushed or loud? Is it actively involved and innovative or tightly regulated and wary? Are these factors helping or hindering your business?

There are additional office management duties to attend to after your environment has been taken into consideration. Through a work-order or tickets system, you may be responsible for managing the technical support staff, security teams, or maintenance personnel both inside and outside. Additionally, you may have to coordinate facility maintenance with your landlord or property manager, make orders for new equipment, and maintain track of your hardware inventory. Although there are many details, one thing is consistent: running an office demands regular supervision and prompt action.

Want to see the team's career progress

While it's admirable to be motivated in your own career, it's crucial for managers to pay attention to the careers of their teams as well. It's crucial to have a passionate attitude towards assisting your team members as they advance along their own career paths, whether they remain with the firm, move into a new function within the organization, or go on to another company entirely.

When people see you as a boss who cares about their growth, it may be quite gratifying at work.

Is your workplace really secure?
It's wise to maintain your building secure from intruders or external danger, whether by keyed entrance or active shooter procedure. Your responsibilities can include directing security teams, keeping an eye on closed-circuit televisions, or giving new hires keys. Similarly, it's crucial that the furnishings and machinery in your workstation are secure to use. Make sure you have thought of every potential threat to your facility and campus and have a strategy to minimize it.

Adept with technology

It's beneficial to understand how technology works. You can have trouble if you're not adept with some of the fundamental programmers, including Microsoft Office and Excel. Being proficient with technology and the usage of online platforms is necessary for managers.

It's a talent that can be picked up, but if you don't already know how to use the tools or software, it will probably need some practice on your side.

Analytical

Finding more effective methods to do the tasks at hand is a part of a manager's job. It's critical to pinpoint any areas in your work where your performance could be poor and figure out how to fix them.

When managing an office setting, having an analytical eye is a useful talent to have. It might help your company save money and provide consumers and clients a better service.

If you're thinking, "How could this be improved?" or 'what can be done to make this more efficient?', you're almost halfway there. It's a good idea to include analytical buzzwords in your CV when applying for a position like this. The terms "problem-solving," "critical thinker," and "optimization" are all excellent choices.

Encourage more learning and growth

Workplace morale may be raised and productivity can be raised by encouraging team members to keep growing and giving them more training chances. Employees may perform more effectively and provide higher-quality output if they are given the opportunity to advance their professional knowledge and abilities.

Additionally, it can put them in a better position for internal promotion. For instance, if you give a marketing assistant a task that needs them to utilize software they aren't acquainted with, think about providing them with tutorials or asking a more experienced worker to teach them how to use the programme. They may then finish the work more quickly and utilise the programme again for subsequent assignments.

These are some helpful tips to keep you going further more ..